THINGS
OF
INTRINSIC
WORTH

by Wallace D. McRae

illustrated by Clinton Y. McRae

Published by: Outlaw Books
                P.O. Box 4466
                Bozeman, MT 59772

Edited by Jeri D. Walton

ISBN # 0-945960-02-6

Other Books by Wally McRae:
It's Just Grass and Water   5.95
Up North is Down the Crick   7.00

Order from Outlaw Books by sending check or money order for book and add $1.50 postage and handling.

CONTENTS

FOREWORD

Probably the best (or worst) comment I could make about Wallace McRae's work is, "It's almost literature." And that is a dangerous precedent for him to be setting in the world of cowboy poetry. Most cowboy poetry is common, as in "She's got a sort'uva common head." Though Wallace's poetry is plain . . . It is seldom common.

I am a friend of Wally's and a fan. Were he not a poet I would still be both. He is a person who takes the world seriously. Even in the poem *The Hired Hand,* which makes me laugh out loud, it ends with his stampin' his foot like an ol' ewe!

Wally's poems seem to ponder things. For the most part they pursue some original thought. I delight in reading his funny stuff to my friends.

But his serious poetry embarrasses me. I've seen him do *Put That Back . . . Hoedown* in public. People smile and laugh and tap their feet. It goes by so fast we're amazed that he can do it by heart. Then I read the bitter words. It's like listening to a man in the electric chair tellin' jokes.

Wallace McRae is a powerful writer with something to say. The last verse of the title poem gives you a sense of what's burnin' inside him. Read it. . . aloud. It's more than just one rancher's cry in the wilderness, it is the anguished wail of civilized man.

Were he from any other country on Earth Wallace McRae would be a national treasure.

Baxter Black

PUNCHER POET PLAGUE

"Bein' a cowboy poet's not easy," so says the
    good Doctor Black.
That's claptrap and Baxter he knows it. For
    there ain't no discernable lack
Of them hokey poke-cow rhymers. They're
    multiplyin' each day!
Why lately I heard this here rumor that Dow has
    developed a spray
That they'll put in the booze down in Elko and
    apply on envelope flaps
That are self addressed back to *Tara and on the
    dice that we use to shoot craps.
Book burners should ban Gail Gardner, Kiskaddon
    and Badger Clark too.
Cow poets are sweepin' the country like the
    scours, viral AIDS, and the flu.
They say Frisco's got gay caballeros. Dallas
    Cowboys call signals in rhyme,
Them buckaroo bunkhouse-bred bards, pard,
    are a plague, like Mafia crime!
We've gone to hell in a basket stamp. Levi
    Strauss peddles blue jeans with verse.
Bein' a cowboy poet's plumb easy. And partner
    she's gonna git worse.
We must all do our part in this crisis since the
    solution is simple, you see:
I urge you to sign this petition banning all
    cowboy poets . . . but me.

*Tara McCarty is the General Manager
of the Cowboy Poetry Gathering in Elko, Nevada.

OUTRIDERS AT THE END OF THE TRAIL

They contemplate their town-boot toes
As they stand around and mill.
They check the south horizon,
'Cross the tracks above the hill.
Their suitcoats hint of mothballs.
Their Levis are clean and creased.
They speak of grass or cattle
But never the deceased.
Some have shook the Gov'ner's hand,
And one's been in the pen.
Crooked legs define the bronc hands,
Cropped off thumbs the dally men.
Their springtoothed necks are throttled up
In silky black wild rags.
Their faces scored like flower-stamps
On well-worn saddle bags.
They've come early to the funeral home,
Yet don't want to go inside.
There's no comfort in a breathless room
Or words of "eventide".
They somehow share a secret bond
As each one recollects:
Together.   Separate.   Silently.
Each pays his last respects.

You'll hear no keening to the vaulted skies,
But the good hands know when a good hand dies.

Dedicated to the memory
of my Uncle Evan D. McRae

SNUFFY AND SODIE AND THE COWBOY CODE

"Now I ain't scared a'grizzly bears,"
    old Snuffy says one day,
"'N wolverines n' catamounts
    to me is pure child's play.
Them trantulas and scorpions?
    I'll prance around 'em bold!
But partner, them dang rattlesnakes,
    they make my blood run cold.
I lariats my bed each night.
    My boots is tall bullhide.
I don't like bein' on the ground,
    shoot yes! That's why I ride.
Despite these nifty safety steps,
    I knows that I'll git bit.
I cogitates on remedies
    to use if I git hit.
My old Case knife is razor sharp
    to slash acrost each hole
Where that bugger's fangs went,
    still, it chills me to the soul
To plan self-mutilation,
    although it's necessary.
'N suckin that there pizen out
    to me is awful scary.
I reckon I could do it, if
    my life was on the line.
'Cause I 'member when that critter bit
    my hoss, Sweet Adeline.
Now that pony was a kicker
    of that there's paltry doubt.
No man on earth could suck *his* leg
    to git the pizen out.

So his eyes they glassied over
    'n sweat jist drenched his hide.
He shuddered, then he staggered,
    'n I stood there as he died.
Sometimes I lays awake at night
    a'ponderin' on this.
'N I gits to speculatin'
    on this hypothesis:
Say now, Sodie, jist fer instance,
    we're out hossback some day
'N old Cookie's beans has grabbed me
    in a most emphatic way,
Now I got no time to tarry,
    no sir! I'm in a rush.
But propriety it dictates
    that I got to find some brush.
Well, I gits there, but jist barely.
    There's no time to scout around.
And say - in this brush's a viper
    all coiled up on the ground.
Now I don't see him, but he sees me
    'n he feels crowded some,
So he calculates trajectory
    'n bites me on the bum.
So here I am all wounded
    but I knows what must be done,
So fishin' out my sharp Case knife,
    I carves X's on my bun.
But this I do by braille, you see.
    I'm operatin' blind.
So I carves out love and kisses
    all over my behind.

But I cain't suck the pizen out
     'cause folks ain't built fer that.
Then I thinks about you, Sodie,
     'n I yells 'n waves my hat.
So you rides up, 'n I tells you
     the awful fix I'm in.
I'm checkin' all my bets to you.
     Jist you can save my skin.
My eyes is glazin' over now.
     My sun is sinkin' fast.
I'm remorseful of my sin-filled life;
     regret my pintoed past.
This nightmare here's well water clear
     I pitcher in my mind.
I'm dyin' there. The question is,
     now, Sodie, could you find
It in yer heart to help a pal
     whose friendship is devout
'N save my life by suckin' all
     that rattler's pizen out?
'Cause the Cowboy Code, it tells
     the obligations of a friend.
It says, I quote, 'A pal must be
     faithful to the end.'"

Well, Sodie rolled and lit a smoke
     and said, 'Yore right about
The Cowboy Code, but it don't
     cover suckin' pizen out.
That 'faithful to the end,' you quote
     I'd say is misdefined.
It dang sure don't require of me
     to tend to yore behind.
If you git bit, I'll fan yer face
     'n help the time pass by.
I'll speak soft words, but pardner,
     yore damn sure gonn'a die!"

LEVIS

Well now Grandpa called 'em "overalls".
While the kids all calls 'em "jeans".
But I disputes old-timers
And folks just in their teens
'Cause a rose by any other name
Just might not be no rose.
So I tells 'em, "I'll take Levis."
When I'm gittin' cowboy clothes.
Oh, there's a hunderd brand names
If you want to take a chance
While punchin' cows out on the range,
Or at a country dance.
But me? I'm right specific,
Ranch or Main Street they're in style.
And I'm partial to my Levis
By at least a country mile.

COWBOY WAGES

Higher salary, or wage, is a current rage
As people whip and spur for the buck.
Down there in town people elbow and frown
And say poor folks are "down on their luck."

But I don't agree. It just seems to me,
That my luck's a lot better than theirs.
High wages to me are riding plumb free
Where the wind cleanses me of my cares.

Let them get their kicks in their canyons
    of bricks.
I'll get mine out here on the range
Where the wages are low, and pace kinda slow
But the jobs and the seasons still change.

THE YELLOWSTONE

Millions of buffalo curried her flanks
  as she shed winter's ice in the spring.
In the smoke of ten thousand campfires
  she heard drum beats and war dances ring.
On the crest of her bosom, she sped Captain Clark
  and Sacajawea as well.
She bisected prairie, the plains and the mountains
  from her birthplace in "John Colter's Hell."
To the trav'ler she whispered, "Come follow me."
  with a wink and a toss of her head.
She tempted the trapper, gold miner and gambler
  to lie down by her sinuous bed.
"Safe passage", she murmured provocatively.
  "Safe passage and riches as well."
She smiled as the thread of Custer's blue line
  followed her trails and then fell.
She carved out the grade for the railroads;
  Took settlers to their new home;
Watered their stock, watered the fields,
  and let them grow crops on her loam.
Her banks were the goal of the trail herds.
  Her grass was the prize that they sought.
'Till the blizzards of 'eighty six and seven
  nearly killed off the whole lot.
"Don't boss her, don't cross her." Let her run free,
  and damn you don't dam her at all.
She's a wild old girl, let her looks not deceive you. . .
  But we love her in spite of it all.

This poem was written at the request of the Montana Department of Highways for use on a Historic Marker located at a rest area on Interstate 94 west of Hysham.

THE SAGA OF WEE DONNIE MacPHIE

"I ken Burn's Nicht's a comin',"
    observes Big Dunc MacKye.
"Sa we best be preparin' tha' it
    dinna slip by."
But Wee Don MacPhie, his partner,
    says wi an unco froon,
"Ye best gae by yoursel tae
    bonny Miles Toon."
"Gae by mysel, Wee Donnie?
    I kinna trust m' ear.
Wha ither sart a blather
    kin I expec tae hear?
Will ye'll say the Pope's a Methydist,
    and all guid sheepdogs bark?
I dinna ken the blather
    or the muckle that I hark.
Ye'll no miss the pipes a skirlin'
    oot wi' a Hielan' tune?"
But Wee Don shrugs, "Gae by youself
    tae bonny Miles Toon."
"Och! I ken ye," chortles Duncan,
    an' winket his right ee,
"Ye're gang in wi' the widow,
    'stead a gang wi' me.
I recollect last Burns Nicht,
    when ye'd had a drap or twa,
An ye reeled and ye shottished
    a' aroon the ha'
We yer airm aroon the widow,
    an' a glimmer in yer ee.
I'll stand aside for love m' lad,"
    says Dunc tae Don MacPhie.

"Ye'r right aboot the widow,"
	Donnie says wi' mournful croon.
"She's the reason that ye'll gae alone
	tae bonny Miles Toon.
I'll stay 'n tend the sheep and dogs;
	and muck the wagon oot.
Ye gae and hae a guid time, Dunc.
	Hae yoursel a toot.
Caus the widow broke both heart and head
	in one fell blaw, I guess.
She boxed m' ear and blacked m' ee
	and straik me merciless."
"Wha did ye tae desairve sich
	abuse upon yer pow?
I kinna ken," says Dunc MacKye,
	"Ye best explyn i' now."

"Well, the widow's na a Scot, ye see."
	begins Wee Don MacPhie.
"So she's got these bonny questions
	that she inquires of me.
I explyns aboot St. Andrew, and Rab Roy
	(by Walter Scott)
'N the heather and the haggis
	and the saary English-lot.
I spaik profoond aboot the unco
	Scottish Queen named Mary
And of our Rab Burns' birthday
	which is late in January.
I spaik of Lochs, of tarns and glens
	and Caledonians
And of the bonny tartans . . . the claes
	of a' the clans.

I minded of m' manners,
    bit m' tongue until it hurt;
When askin' of m' claes and garb,
    she called m' kilt a skirt!
Kindly-like I told her that the kilt
    was its right name,
And that pantaloons were hated back
    in our Hielan' hame.
I told her of the thistle,
    the sporrans and the durks,
The Glengarrys, the pies
    and of haunted Scottish kirks.
M' pow was a' a'swarmin'.
        M' heart was a' afire.
I crowed and glowed and preened—
    like a cock atop the byre . . .
Like the beastie 'pon our Scottish flag;
    I was a rampant lion.
The widow was agog wi' me,
    a' fluttery and sighin'.
Wi' a sheep's eye then she asked me,
    her voice a golden gilt,
'Is anything, dear Donald,
    worn beneath your kilt?'
I may hae been too honest
    considering m' fate;
Because when I answered,
    she began to straik m' pate.
Lang and deep I'd pondered 'til I told her
    wi' a grin,
'I would say there's naught what's wore.
    I'd say well broken in!'"

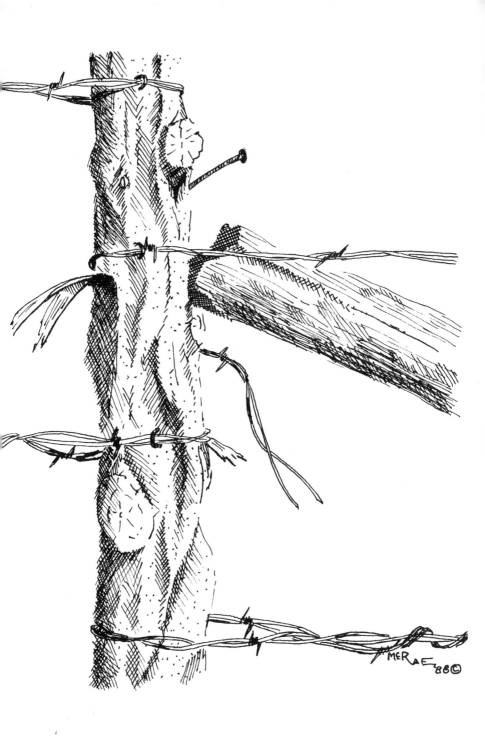

A SALUTE TO THE COWBOY ARTISTS

Cowboys learned how to ride from their daddies
On some wore-out gentle ranch hoss.
Cowboys learned how to cry from their mothers,
Or a rough-hewn old rawhide range boss.

The Code of the West came from movies.
John Wayne taught the saunterin' walk.
"Smile, when you call me that, stranger."
Owen Wister taught cowboys to talk.

Kindly whores and country school teachers
Gave lessons on love and on sex.
Cow punchers got safety instructions
From numerous horse and cow wrecks.

But who taught us "Laugh Kills Lonesome"?
Or be ready when "Horses Talk War..."
It wasn't Zane Grey (though we read him);
And it sure wasn't Louis L'Amour.

But we learned to appreciate sunsets
And the beauty of unspoiled range.
And maybe we learned - call it tolerance-
For cultures that at first seemed strange.

We learned hist'ry from calendar pictures.
Yes, we learned how to act and to dress,
For the values, the gear and the costumes
Seeped from canvas to subconsciousness.

Now, ev'ry cowboy that loves this old West
Has a trace of oil paint in his veins.
When the last cowboy's bones are paved over
Your record'll be all that remains

In bronze and painted on canvas,
So that "civilzation" can say,
"This was the life of the cowboy.
He sure gave her hell in his day."

So here's thanks from your friends, Cowboy Artists,
We used your talents as a matter of course
As you captured forever, an era
Of the West and a man and a horse.

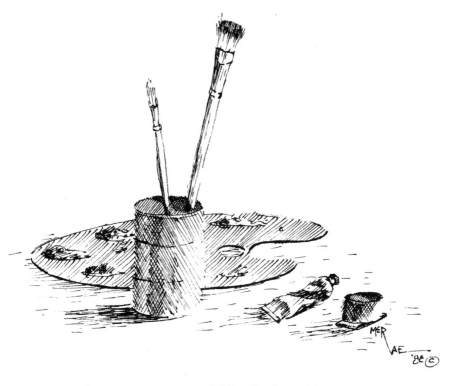

CHARLES FINLEY PARKINS

The coroner come callin'
    to the Parkins place last week.
He loaded Charlie Finley up
    and hauled him down the creek.

Some folks thought Fin was loco,
    sorta cross-wired in the head,
But me, I kinda liked him
    and now that he is dead
I get to thinkin' 'bout him.
    Was he different? To the bone.
He somehow always was a child
    even when full grown.
They say that scarlet fever
    stole away his hearing.
His ma protected little Fin
    and passed to him her fearing
Of what the world would do to him.
    From life he was withdrawn.
He was an idle pauper prince;
    both dilettante and pawn.
He never did a lick of work.
    (Well, maybe just some trifle.)
Mostly slipped around the countryside
    with a rimfire rifle.
The butt of mean and nasty jokes
    was all the note he got.
It beat invisibility, I guess,
    but not a lot.
He never rode or drove a car
    or had a lady friend

Or smoked or drank or swore.
    Fin was saintly to the end
Yet he never had religion,
    though he never raised no hell.
And when he died the neighbors said,
    "It's prob'ly just as well,
He had a long and easy life.
    It was time for him to go."
It seems to me that old Fin died
    some eighty years ago.

But . . .
The coroner come callin'
    to the Parkins Place last week
And loaded Charlie Finley up,
    and hauled him down the creek.

APPLIED GENESIS

. . . And God said unto man: "Be fruitful, and multiply, and replenish the earth, and subdue it, and have dominion over the fish of the sea, and over the fowl of the air, and over every living thing that moveth upon the earth." Genesis 1:28
"I'm hereby designating you
 to serve as my straw boss."
God said, "You're on my payroll,
 so get to work now, Hoss.
You whip them critters into shape.
 Make 'em do whate're you bid.
Just point 'em where you wanta go.
 Let your ego shape their id."

But a coyote's independent.
 He just don't seem inclined
To stand no domination.
 And them skunks? They never mind.
It aught to be plumb easy
 to forbid a hoss to buck.
Though I've choked the horn right prayerful
 I ain't had a lotta luck.
'N I been bit 'n struck 'n kicked
 more times 'n I can count
By hosses, so my bossin' don't
 seem so paramount.
There's staphs and streptococci
 (all them doobies you can't see)
That I can't keep throwed in a herd.
 They pay no mind to me.

Them lice 'n grubs 'n horn flies
    rattlesnakes and prairie dogs
Are what you'd call free spirits.
    They ignore my monologs.
"I don't mean to sound important,"
    I told this longhorn steer,
"But I'm yer boss." He got me down
    and walked off half my ear.
"Let's get this straight," I told this hen,
    "I'm boss here! Understand?
Them eggs is mine! Get off 'em."
    and she pecked me on the hand.

I'm right proud of my position
    and this awesome job I hold.
But all them beasts 'n fish 'n fowl
    musta not been told
I'm s'posed to ramrod all them beasts
    on land, in air and sea.
But the earth and all her critters
    has got dominion over me.

CUSTER COUNTRY

This is a land of grass and pine,
    of ash and cottonwood
That the natives of the region call
    "piva", "bot sots" and "good".
It's the Yellowstone and Yellowtail
    yellow sandstone soaring high;
And cattle and coal and history
    beneath an azure sky.
The land of the Crow and Cheyenne too;
    the land that Custer trod.
It's a land of subtle beauty
    deep-rooted in prairie sod.

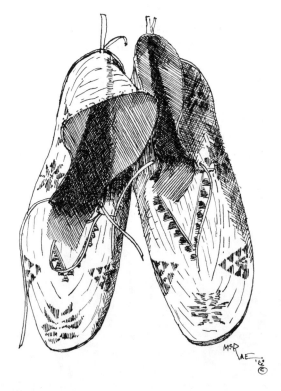

THE SUBSTITUTE

"I shore don't worry 'bout fake beef."
Says a feller down the road.
As he rassles with a plastic sack
Of urea from his load.

"It's plain to me, Americans
Just won't accept no fraud."
He says as he sips fruitade,
And I shrug and sorta nod.

"No scientist can reproduce
The texture and the taste,
Of beef", he says while coating bread
With oleomargarine paste.

He stirs saccharin in his cup,
And gestures with a match,
Just struck with difficulty,
Upon a nylon patch.

He kicks a butyl tire, as he
Punctuates his thunder.
"You're prob'ly right." I then agree.
(But still, I sometimes wonder.)

THE OLD COWBOY SONG

What the hell's become of the old cowboy song,
With that easy and slow runnin' walk kinda beat?
And them lyrics 'bout trailin' them trail herds along
'Neath the starry sky? They was simple and sweet.

Have the Pioneers' Sons caressed their last chord;
Or Eddie sung out the last cattle call?
Marty Robbins has claimed his final reward.
And the Bad Brahma Bull has died in a stall.

Old Paint's last tracks led out of Cheyenne.
But where was he headed? Well, folks can't agree.
Some say he was rustled in a U-Haulit Van
Or his ashes were scattered in west Tennessee.

I've heard that the genes of The Strawberry Roan,
And some of the get of the old Zebra Dun
Got crossed-up with Elvis, or a Hank Williams moan,
So that Country, not Cowboy 's become number one.

Now ballads tell about eighteen wheelers
With two-speed Brownies and cabover Petes.
'Stead of tear-jerkin' tales of smashed bronc peelers,
We get boozers and losers and tangled bed sheets.

Long, so long gone is the old cowboy song
That shuddered and died as "Country" got bigger.
Gotta get along without "little dogies git along."
The new Nashville nuance has got hybrid vigor.

So now pool rooms, prisons and pawn shops are hot
While pore "Joe the Wrangler" has died, at least twice.
Hear them bang the drum loudly over love gone to pot?
They don't sing about critters, but of glitter and vice.

But wait a dang minute. Haul back on them reins.
They're still playin' songs for the people who ride.
Red Steagal's still doin' old Bob Wills' refrains,
And sometimes George Strait's genuine cowboyfied.

The Bunkhouse Band's been hittin' the road.
Horse Sense is out on another world tour.
World Champion LeDoux still ain't been throwed
And thousands of bars is cowboy song poor.

McMahan's still kickin' the last that I heard.
And Ohrlin still cusses that confounded wheel.
Ranger Doug and The Riders keep pointin' the herd.
And Tyson still sings 'em just like we feel!

So the old cowboy song is alive and plumb well;
Just a'spurrin' and scratchin' and raisin' a fuss.
The only dang reason it ain't bigger 'n hell
Is that cow country Deejays don't know about us!

THE CAMPAIGN SPEECH

The politician was orating,
Not only loud, but long.
Two punchers stood rumenating
Among the listening throng.

One of the two was carryin' some age.
And was more than a little "deef".
Indicating the feller up on the stage,
Asked his pal, "Now what's his beef?

"What the hell is he givin' hell
And oratin' on today?"
The other replied with a thoughtful, "Well
Don't know. So far, he don't say."

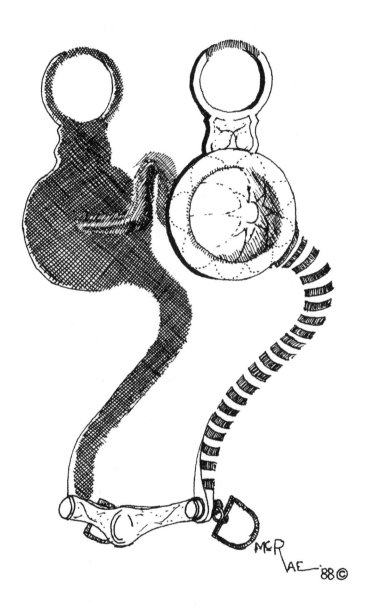

PUT THAT BACK...HOEDOWN

Start tapping your foot in 4/4 time and read this as if you're calling a square dance. If you really have trouble with the beat, just give Wally a call and he'll recite a small portion for you.

Supercolliders, M H D,
    and coal-fired powerplants.
The fiddles croon; sweet is the tune.
    Now everybody dance.
For it's jobs, growth and money,
    and a song the band can play;
We'll revel through the midnight hours
    until the break of day.
Now balance with your partner
    and the gal across the hall,
For Alamand's left the cowboy life
    and he's gonna have a ball.
Promenade all to the Union Hall.
    Get hand-stamped there for life.
Sashay out with benefits for you,
    your kids and wife.
Right hand across to the MX pad.
    Tell Ivan, "Howdy-do."
Left hand back with lead gloves on
    and, "General, how are you?"
Shimmy down in a Texas Star,
    with a chain saw in your hand,
And clear-cut trees two centuries old
    to McCulloch's Ragtime Band.
Hum, hum uranium.
    Oh hear them Geigers rattle.
This beats to hell, any-old-day,
    them days with longhorn cattle.

Buy a modern box lunch. Pay a bunch
    for a Hostess Twinkie, pard.
Promenade with Gatorade.
    and puke out in the yard.
Now, do-si-do a Case backhoe
    for another septic tank.
And two-step to your Harley too
    and climb a spoil bank.
Put yer little foot down. Don't be slow.
    Hear them hydraulics whine.
Another day. The pay ain't hay
    in the mother-lovin' mine.
Them power lines hum at all times
    from here down to L.A.
Turkey in the straw. Change that law
    to make them hummers pay.
Pay the gent thirty percent.
    Too much? We'll cut her down
To an itty bitty pittance,
    or they'll close down my hometown.
Town and country get along,
    or we'll condemn your ranch,
'Cause meat it comes from IGA.
    Now everybody dance.
Dance around the outside.
    Boil that cabbage down.
Wheat and cows and sheep don't pay?
    Then ship yer kids to town.
We'll pay them dough, boy, dough, boy, dough.
    And you can sell the farm.
Or put it in the CRP.
    It won't do any harm.
Harm onee is good for me and you
    and her and him.
Chicken in the bread pan
    pickin' out dough and palladium,

Platinum and chromate ore.
     Watch out!....Another truck!
Lucky thing we come yer way.
     Oh, lucky Lady Luck!
Oh! Looky here the old coon dog
     has done laid down and died.
They're mining copper once again
     across that big divide.
Divide and conquer. Left and right,
     split right down the middle.
Cotton-eyed Joe and do-si-do.
     Now let's hear that fiddle.
Fiddle again with big BN
     and they won't haul yer grain.
Massa's on the cold cold ground.
     I'm bucked off in the rain.
Reinin' left. Reinin' right,
     on my reinin' hoss;
Hired hand up and quit today.
     Now who'll be my boss?
Circle two-step. Circle wagons.
     Who's the Circle jerk?
Minors packin' fake I.D.'s.
     Miners outa work.
Workin' on the railroad
     all the live-long day.
Skin the Cat. Dog the steer.
     Take Chapter Twelve today.
It's polka dot in the old oil spot
     as we poke that drill bit down.
Varsouvian on the old hardpan;
     then hoedown down downtown.
Chicken Reel 'n how ya feel
     as we rip across The West?
Turkey Trot in the new mall lot
     with the gal you love the best.

Let's all join hands and Circle West,
    and let the moon shine in.
Let down yer hair and rip and tear,
    destruction ain't no sin.
Now Home Sweet Home to the mobyle home,
    (a 'sixty-nine New Moon.)
Crank up the Ford. Don't be bored,
    just hum a cowboy tune.
Thank the boys with 'lectric toys
    that played the country dance.
Though there's damn little Country left,
    pay your money, take yer chance.
The Country Dance ain't got no chance
    if Mother Earth's a whore.
Heel and toe and away we go.
    Goin'...Gone.
            There ain't no more.

LITTLE THINGS

I've laid for hours upon my back
Just looking at the sky,
At clouds; or if the sky was clear,
The motes within my eye.
D'jever spend an hour or more
Just staring at the crick?
Or a scarab roll a ball of dung?
Or ants rass'lin' with a stick?
Or, on a cloudy-windy day,
See a windmill seem to fall?
Or stop stock still with neck hairs raised
By a plaintive coyote call?
Swallows slice their swaths across
The sky like scimitars.
I'm humbled by the intricate
Snowflakes' prismic stars.
I've laughed as stove-up killdeer
Go a'-scrabblin' 'cross a draw.
I've seen cedar trees explode in flames
As I'm consumed with awe.
Arms crossed and leaning forward
Weight on the saddle horn,
I'm a fascinated crowd of one;
A calf is being born.

The measure of your intellect,
The learn-ed people say,
Are the things that fascinate us.
They're a mental expose´.
You got to be dang careful
If you want to be thought smart,
And keep sorta confidential
Little things that's in your heart.

STAMPEDE

"You cowboys are so glamorous
Your life's so wild and free."
"But," the lady said, "this question
Has just occurred to me.
There surely is one thing in life
That all you cowboys fear.
If you'll excuse impertinence,
I'd dearly love to hear
Just what it is that frightens you
And chills you to the bone.
Is it wild broncs or rattlesnakes
Or dying all alone?"
Though all of those were dangerous
The cowpoke said that he'd
Always thought the scariest
Was a genuine stampede.
"Though our cattle are more do-cile
Than they used to be,
The potential for disaster
Scares the liver outa me."
The lady said, "A stampede then
Is the thing that you most fear,
Can you have a stampede, sir,
That just involves one steer?"
The cowboy's mental gears wound up
And then he dropped the clutch,
"Why sure, one critter can stampede,
But he cain't scatter much!"

ON THE PAUCITY OF PRIME PUNCHERS

The country's full-up with cowboys
    that never hit their lick.
The time between bein' too green
    and too old... was too damn quick.

GOOSEBERRIES

Gooseberry bushes with hostility bristle
To prickle your imprudent hands.
Their alum-sour fruit will burgle your whistle-
Assaulting your maxilla glands.

Gooseberry bushes are uncommonly common.
Few sponsors their praises will sing.
For a bit each year they gladden the land,
The first greening leaves of the spring.

CHARLIE BLACK

Who was it killed poor Charlie Black
In his wagon long ago?
Was it some Indian passer-by
Or some Caucasian foe?

Whose sheep did Charlie Black tend?
Was it Baringer or Smith?
Who found Charlie Black's still form?
Had Charlie kin or kith?

Who laid Charlie Black to rest
Near the head of Miller Creek?
Who piled the stones upon his grave
Out under Garfield peak?

Damn little's known of Charlie Black
The mysteries are rife.
We know he died, but no one knows
One thing about his life.

THE BALLAD OF THE NOT SO EASY RIDER

I'm in a saloon perched on a stool
Lyin' and laughin' just like a fool,
When a pall fell on the assembled multitude.
So I looked around to see just why
Our party suddenly seemed to die,
And I sees this great big scruffy biker-dude.

He wore a head-rag like old Willie
'N a Levi coat that looked plumb silly
'Cause the arms was gone; and so was parta one ear.
He wore chains and studs and a Nazi cross,
And I was sorta at a loss
To figger out why this biker showed up here:

In a cowboy bar. But I didn't care.
I always practiced laissez faire,
As long as a stranger kept his horns pulled in.
"Live 'n let live." says the Code of the West.
So, usually, I never messed
With folks. 'Cause bein' diff'rent ain't no sin.

But this Harley hand was loud and rank.
'N he opined as he swore and drank,
On things that damn sure went again' my grain.
He cussed them "Pimps" and "Wimps" and "Wops",
The FBI and assorted cops
And women with words both graphic and profane.

Though he was big and rank and mean,
And looked as tough as a threshin' machine,
My duty was plain as the hairs on his nose to see.
I had to defend the Code of the West,
Subdue this varmit; destroy this pest.
Make him recant his evil words on bended knee.

I'd be like Rambo and Lash Larue,
Harrison Ford and John Wayne too.
I'd slay Goliath, just like David done.
He'd soon go crashin' to the floor,
'N say, "Enough, you won this war."
He'd cringe and cower as humble as a nun.

Folks'd say, "Ol' Wally, he done good.
He's a hero in this neighborhood."
Or, "He never cut that biker any slack."
Course I'd be modest-like and shy
As they praised me to the sky,
'N bought a round, and clapped me on the back.

Yes sir! Then outa' my reverie,
I sees this monster approachin' me,
So I silently says, "Come on, make my day."
Then he says to me, "You cowboy creep,
How come it is you smell like sheep?"
Then I says back, "Any....Anything you say!"

Yep, Let Lash Larue or Sly Rambo,
Or John Wayne give this dude a go.
But me? I won't offend him. Nope, no way!
It wouldn't take no dietarian
To know he ain't no vegetarian.
He'd prob'ly eat a side a'beef a day.

Oh, I coulda took him. Ain't no doubt.
But I'd prob'ly scattered his teeth about,
Er maybe killed him. Which'd been a mistake.
Them carnivore ranks is already thin;
We need meat-eaters just like him!
So I turned him loose to let him propagate.

THE BALING SYNDROME

Three or four knots are hung on the bill hook.
The twine finger's got a hangnail.
The hay dog has got his tongue hanging out.
The clouds in the west look like hail.

The pickup is sure getting smooth-mouthed.
The hydraulic tension's relaxed.
It seems that I've broken some more feeder tines,
Since the last two bales just prolapsed.

A whirlwind just carried some windrows away,
Depositing them in the creek.
And then, just before the shear bolt sheared off,
The needles were "plunged" like a streak.

Two miles from home. Here comes the rain.
My tractor distributor's wet. . .
If you've never baled on one of those days,
Then you've never been to Hell . . . yet!

COWBIRDS

Like lazy lilies of the field,
They neither toil nor spin.
They put their kids in foster homes
Which seems to some a sin.

They seem to lack a conscience
Concerning child abandonment.
As they casually chase pleasure
Self-indulgent and content.

Alated nanny substitutes
Let them lout about.
The Jet Set thinks that cowbirds
Have life all figured out.

THE BROKEN SPELL

Walt Evans and Jimmie Peppers and me
Rode in a fog one day, half lost.
'Til the sun exchanged the mystery
Of mists, for a landscape of frost.

Each blade of grass was as big as your thumb,
Each pine an explosion of white.
In silence we rode, by beauty struck dumb,
Absorbing the visual delight.

Then two deer walked out in a crystal glade,
Perfecting the panoramic view.
And Peppers burst out with this accolade,
"Gol damn boys, ain't that pitcher Q?"

DEFINITIONS OF "POOR"

We was dirt-poor in the 'thirties and 'forties,
Though I didn't know it back then,
'Cause it seemed we was rich when we went to the store
In town, every now and again.
We'd buy sugar and flour in hunderd pound sacks,
Plain ones, not calico-dyed.
(Them calico prints was a dead give-away.
Mom sewed white ones. She had her pride.)
We'd buy oatmeal in Quaker Oat tom toms
That musta been *this* big around,
Hills Brothers, Yella boxes of soda,
Nuts in a sack by the pound.
And Dad'd get four pairs a' stiff overalls.
Mom'd get wicks for the lamps,
And some mantles for the one in the front room,
And clothespins with fancy wire clamps.
We'd get kerosene, bluing and vinegar,
And salt (with that girl in the rain)
Lime and rivets, a keg of staples, pine tar,
Stoveblack and a length of tug chain.
The girls'd each get a hair ribbon apiece.
And Dad'd get Mom a new comb.
My prize was a bottle of or'nge Knee Hi
That I'd sip on, half the way home.
Just after he'd got his caddy of Durham,
Dad'd ask, "Charge it 'till fall?"
"You bet." comes back the answer, "Those steers gonna
Break down the scales in St. Paul?"

Did I say we was poor? I think of them years
Way back there in my memory.
But a poor cow was hungry, so we wasn't poor.
At least that's what Dad said to me.
He said, "Sick cows is poor, while we're healthy;
And cows can get poor in a storm.
But we got a house and a stove and wood pile,
And hunderds of ways to keep warm."
"What's rich then?" I asks him. He says, "It means fat."
Then I asks him, "Ain't we sorta lean?"
"No, we're right in the middle between fat and poor.
Yep, right smack-dab there in-between!"

Of course Dad was playin' semantical games;
And foolin' with me. He'd confess.
But I think he was right. We was there in the middle
Between "poor" and "fat" . . . more or less.

PAX VOBISCUM

My hired hand quit the other day
Greener fields to graze.
He's packed and gone. His saddle rack
Is vacant to my gaze.

His house filled just with memories;
My footsteps echo now.
His string of horses idle stand.
They miss him too somehow.

No longer does his dog's clear bark
Announce our company.
No peal of laughter from his kids
Now breaks my reverie.

I see the country that we rode,
The calf we pulled at dawn,
The coffee pot whose brew we shared,
His quiet empty lawn.

A snoose can now reflects my stare,
As empty as my heart.
May peace be with you, Mike, my friend,
Though we be miles apart.

DOCK GROOM

I see a yeller Studebaker
    easin' down the crick.
Ol Dock, 'n 'Ceil, 'n Ruthie
    has got some plums to pick.
I bet Ruthie's grinin' in the back,
    while up front is Dock and 'Ceil.
You'd think they was a family,
    but naw, that ain't the deal.
Carl Whitaker is Ruthie's dad,
    and 'Ceils Carl's wife.
And Carl is prob'ly Dock's best friend;
    has been all his life.
But mostly Carl he stays to home
    a'putterin' aroun'
While Dock 'n 'Ceil 'n Ruthie
    goes motorin' to town.
Pore Ruthie's never been all there
    since back when she was foaled,
An' she must be, well let's see now,
    some forty-odd years old.
It's nice of Dock to haul them 'round
    and Carl don't cause no strife.
It prob'ly tickles old Dock some
    when folks think 'Ceil's his wife.
Carl and Dock is trappers, see,
    been partners now for years.
They've caught a thousand coyotes,
    I suppose, in their careers.
I reckon most the headdresses
    the Cheyennes wear was made
From eagles and from ermine,
    that they got from Dock in trade.

Dock used to do livetrappin'
    but he got too old fer that.
He caught a pure white porcupine
    and hunerds of bobcat.
Dock hunts and traps the year around.
    Some folks don't think that's right.
But he's never been on welfare,
    Prides hisself on livin' light.
"There's worlds a coyotes, kid," Dock says.
    And I reckon he should know.
Except fer Dock, his breed died out
    a hunderd years ago.
He runs his traplines nowadays
    in a Studebaker Lark.
At the signposts of gentility
    he sniffed, and left his mark.

Dock's got a tarp and buckets
    piled in the car-top rack.
He and 'Ceil both give a wave.
    Ruthie's grinnin' there in back.

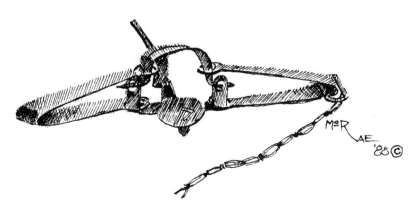

HIRED HAND

You know, some men just look like a cowboy,
Though you'd be hard-pressed to say why.
It may be their posture, or bearing,
Or the confident look in their eye.

Since I was needing some ranch help,
I tapped into the cowboy grapevine,
Where every saloon and each bunkhouse
Can transmit, or receive, on the line.
Later on, well, in rolls this pickup
With them buckin' hoss Wyoming plates,
'N the hat that the driver was wearing
Looks like a twin of George Strait's.
There's rawhide mudflaps on the outfit
And a big goose-neck ball in the back,
A bedroll, a basket-stamped A-fork;
The gun rack's plumb festooned with tack.
On the windshield's a Quarter Horse sticker
From clear back in 'seventy seven.
"Mighty nice country." 's the first words he spoke,
"It sure looks to be a cow heaven.
I was down at the sale barn in Sturgis
Where I hears that yer needin' a hand,
So I drives up through Bell Fourche and Lame Deer
Maybe thinkin' to ride for yer brand.
I'm no hell of a hand now, you savvy?"
(Here he offers a pinch of his snoose.)
"There's lotsa good hands in the country
'N I'm just a sorry excuse.
But all I been's just a cowboy.
I follered a cow all my life.
I guess if I'd been more agressive
I'd maybe still have me a wife.

I lost her 'n them cows, I guess nine years ago.
She called loosin' our cows the last straw.
She called me a loser, (prob'ly she's right,)
And moved back with the mother-in-law.
As a hand goes, I guess I'm just av'rage,
Or maybe a notch below that.
I'm partial t'wards lady-broke horses
That couldn't buck off a man's hat.
Now some people brag on their ropin'
That can't find their way outa town.
Me? If I can't catch 'em runnin',
I keep chargin' until they lay down.
I'd say I'm a lousy horseshoer;
'N machinery I don't cotton to.
Do I drink? Well I ain't no abstainer
'N I like to hoist me a few."
He went on a jokin' and jobbin'
With a humorous gleam in his eye.
Damned if I didn't right away find myself
Laughin' and likin' this guy.
I'd had it with all of them blowhards
With them buckles proclaiming them "Champ".
He could roll out his bed in the bunkhouse;
Diogenes could hang up the lamp.
Here for damn sure was the last honest man,
Who was humble—devoid of all guile.
I figured that here was a cowboy
That could do it all...with a smile.

I was led like a poddy to slaughter.
I'm amazed, 'n I bet you are too.
The sumbitch was a liar, I tell ya,
Ev'ry word that he told me was true!

PIONEER'S VISION

We must nurture this land with a gentle hand;
Look its hardships square in the eye.
We will carve a place, time can not erase,
Between the mountains and the sky.

Come along with me t'wards this vision I see,
It's a vision I have for this land.
From sweat and toil, from our seeds in the soil
Will grow roots, where a nation will stand.

CHRISTMAS

The wood smoke rises t'wards the stars
  As stillness fills the land.
    The drifts reflect the moon's cold beams,
      Stark trees like sentries stand.

The house logs snap with protest
  As if they were in pain.
    Icy ferns and crystal fingers
      Etch o'er the window pane.

But in the house, and in the heart
  There's naught of winter's chill
    But inner warmth that manages
      Both home and soul to fill.

For on this Christmas morning
  We're sheltered by the Birth
    And warmed in body, heart and soul
      By peace upon The Earth.

LIES

Friends and neighbors, I'm a' standin' here
To say there's more lies every year
A'floatin' out across the countryside
These ain't white lies. They're big and black.
Why, Pinocchio'd have to take a back-
Seat to some of these pros who'll lie you
    goggle-eyed.

Like: "D.U.I., Sir? I ain't tight,
Only had two beers to drink tonight."
Or, "Them horse trailer lights was on
    when I left home."
"That pickup's never burnt no oil,
Got bran'-new hubs, rear-end an' coil."
Or, "That ain't leafy spurge, it's
    Lincoln brome."

"Darlin', I'll respect you!" "Interest free."
"Lower your taxes? Just vote for me."
"He seems a little cinchy, but he's never bucked
    one jump!"
"These bulls all gained three pounds a day."
"That quoted price was for yesterday."
"That ain't splints er ringbone, he just
    got that little bump."

"Cain't b'lieve my calf's on yer cow."
"I'll pay you back. That's a solemn vow."
"I really don't believe you when you say
    the kid is mine."
"Ain't never hunted without permission."
"Ol' Blue don't bite! He's above suspicion!"
"I doubt we'll ever mine the coal, just sign
    on this here line."

"No, Nixon never got my vote."
"You never got that check I wrote?"
I could go on and on, but I think you understand.
But the biggest lie I ever heard
Was said by a bureaucratic bird:
"I'm here from the gover'ment and I'll lend
  you folks a hand."

BOX ELDERS

A box elder's a plumb sorry tree
That lays down as it grows.
It genuflects on gouty knees
To wind and wet spring snows.

Its git up and go has gone and went.
It's mighty shy of spunk.
Its branches are arthritic-bent.
Its spine is weak with punk.

Poor lowly kin of cottonwood,
Of stately pine and ash.
A warty dwarf - misunderstood,
A sylvan poor white trash.

With hearts as red as heroes' blood,
(Though no medals grace their breast)
Supine, their trunks defy the flood
With nonviolent protest.

The creek bank's stitched with double seam
Of box elders, slouched at ease.
Hipshot, faithful . . . calm work team . . .
Faithful country trees.

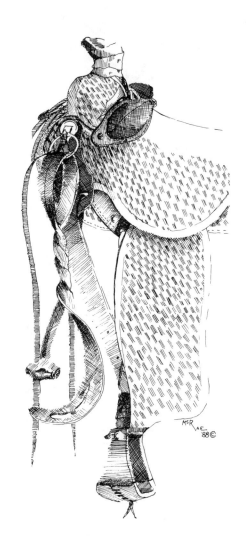

FORKIN' THE INEVITABLE

My horse's back is as cold as this
    October rain.
He's ready, all quiv'rin' and gant.
There's some doubt in my mind whether
    I'll get him rode.
As for him? He *knows* that I can't.

RODEO

Here we go, to the rodeo,
For a rousing rollicking time.
To drink a beer, and give a cheer
For the go-round's fastest time.

Cheer the spills, and all the thrills,
Of the bucking horse, and bull.
Join the throaty roar, that beats down o'er
The arena, from bleachers full.

There's the crushing hush, the heady rush,
For a bull rider that is down.
Then comes relief, saved from the grief,
He's snatched from harm by the clown.

We'll cheer the chaps, in flashing chaps,
And cheer for the critters they ride.
The girls barrel race. There time and space
Are combined and personified.

The lariats smoke, as ropers rope
At the horns, and then at the heels.
Calf horses slide, as their riders glide
To the calf, as he cartwheels.

Kids get their fill. They eat and swill
Hotdogs, and strawberry pop.
Clouds in the west give rumbling protest.
We're shocked by a lone raindrop.

Each calf's been tied. The re-rides tried.
And here comes a man with a broom.
Back home we'll go, from the rodeo,
Once the kids have hit the bathroom.

Each nose has a burn. We no longer yearn
To be part of the rodeo clique.
It's been a thrill, but we've had our fill
Of cowboys . . . at least for a week.

ON RURAL RELOCATION

"Ranch home wanted for large dog," say the ads.
And "Cute kittens need a farm home."
"My city kid's got bad companions,
Needs hard work, and country to roam."

You'd send us all of your paranoid pets.
And the sad, frightened critters you birth.
The kids and the kittens, the rejects and dregs.
Yes, get them back to earth.

But we don't need your problem kids, cats and dogs.
Your delinquents, rejects and such.
We've got problems enough out here on the ranch.
So thanks, but no thanks very much.

John Williams, whose son is married to our daughter, and I conspired and collaborated on this poem. John read it at a retirement roast for Paul Scotten upon Mr. Scotten's retirement as vice president of Montana Power Company at Colstrip, Montana. It contains elements of truth.

PAUL SCOTTEN AND THE TURKEY GAME

Paul Scotten is a legend.
    He's a hero of this age.
Before he hangs his hardhat up
    and turns that final page,
I feel we should reflect a bit
    upon his strongest suit.
His prowess as a hunter
    was known far and wide in Butte.
They tell a tale in Walkerville:
    When Paul took down his gun
That all the game (both beast and fowl)
    pulled out, and at a run.
For all the mighty stags and bulls
    and rams had heard of Paul.
On winter nights they told of him,
    And all the young would bawl.
Game managers still shake their heads
    in awestruck admiration
That Paul could singlehandedly
    trigger fall migration.

Paul shot the mighty grizzly bear.
    Whole herds of elk he slew.
The polar bear, gigantic moose,
    and several caribou,
Some antelope, jack rabbits,
    mountain goats and desert ram,
Their heads all grace his wall above
    a brass plate monogram.
His lifetime trophy list includes
    some things unorthodox:
A windmill, some "No Hunting" signs
    and Kluver's mail box,
A warden's tire, three pickup hoods,
    a gut-shot volleyball.
If it flew or ran or just sat there,
    our Paul had shot 'em all!
Then one fall day it dawned on Paul
    that hunting luck was quirky,
In all the gore and carnage,
    he had never bagged a turkey.
So, I was summoned, and Paul said,
    "Now, John, I'm in a fix.
I want to get a turkey from
    the ranch called Rocker Six.
A gobbler is a stupid bird,
    I've come to understand.
The challenge would be shooting
    on pristine, protected land.
A résumé review disclosed
    that you're most qualified
To seek out Wally's turkeys. John,
    I want you for my guide.
You've got mysterious playthings
    that squawk and squeal and bray
And our records show that, somehow,
    you're an in-law of McRae.

Now John, I'm just a simple man
      and my requests are few.
You like your job? It's settled then.
      I'm sure you will come through."
"But Paul," I said, "Please understand
      this ain't no lead-pipe cinch.
If things go smooth as silk, you still
      might freeze or choke or flinch.
Buck fever's always possible,
      and turkey hunting's tough."
Paul said, "I've got some calls to make,
      besides, I've heard enough!
Turkey shooting's tough, you say?
      Now, John, that's pure bull feces.
If Taylors' ammo just holds out,
      I might wipe out the species!"

I'll dispense with all the details
      of our great turkey quest.
Let's just say that Scotten
      wasn't at his very best.
I won't tell of forty gobblers
      that charged with confidence,
Or of Paul's smoking empty gun
      he swung in self-defense.
You ask, "How did turkey puckey
      end up atop Paul's shoe?"
My lips are sealed. You ask him.
      I'll leave it up to you.
If Paul had been a Pilgrim,
      although it seems absurd,
At Thanksgiving we'd eat pine trees
      and not the noble bird.
No score was kept for wiley birds,
      or for our hunting hero.
A guess? Well, turkeys, fifty-six...
      and Paul Scotten...zero.

SOLD TO THE HIGHEST BIDDER

"Sold to the highest bidder!"
The gavel crashes down.
Another rural family
Goes shamblin' into town.

Sold to the highest bidder,
Their dreams go down, dirt-cheap;
Where every dream's a nightmare
Endured in fitful sleep.

Sold to the highest bidder
The trinkets forged with tears,
Framed pictures on the bureau
Of graduation years.

Sold to the highest bidder.
To town go the crocks and jars,
Just knick-knacks now, or planters
In condos or fern bars.

Sold to the highest bidder,
The cowbell and milk pail.
"They're chic," observes a shallow voice,
"I'll hang them on a nail."

"Sold to the highest bidder!"
The gavel crashes down.
Another rural family
Goes shamblin' into town.

CALL YOURSELVES WHATEVER YOU WANT, (BUT LEAVE ME OUT OF IT)

The Cowbelle title is passe´.
They're now called Cattle Women.
I'll rein around that wild foray
(Though with opinions brimmin'.)

> I'll bite my tongue and write my verse,
> Please spare me from your cursin's.
> They'll find they've gone from bad to worse.
> Will they next be Bovine Persons?

THE DEBUT

Well now, Gillie told this story, so on its truth
    you can't rely,
Since them sainted sons of Erin is a bit inclined
    to lie.
But this is how he told it, so I'll leave it up to
    you;
It may be bull or blarney, then again it might
    be true.

Seems there was this trav'lin' road show come
    rollin' into town
To stage a melodrama. But one dramatist was down
With the grippe or the consumption or a case of
    green gomboo.
But whichever was the ailment, it laid low the
    ingenue.
But the part was just a smidgen (some paltry
    lines, I guess.)
So the ramrod of the road show says, "We ain't in
    no big mess.
I'll just singlefoot up Main Street, and hold me
    an audition
To fill the vacancy in our dramatic composition."

So after he'd explained the deal to the first
    prospect he met,
And asked her if she'd lend a hand, she answered,
    "Yes, you bet."
The lady tried her costume, her few lines and
    learned the plot,
And was nonplussed to discover that she was to be
    shot
By the evil villainess, (who fired a gun with
    blanks).
"No problem." says the lady, "It sounds like fun.
    And thanks."

Well, that same night the Lyceum hummed with
    expectation,
Though the "Patrons of the Arts" was mostly
    cowboys on vacation.
They'd drunk their share of Tiger Tears, so with
    spirits unrestrained,
Their two-bit entry fee insured that they'd be
    entertained.
With rapt anticipation they watched the plot unfold
Betwixt the noble hero and the villain, vile and
    cold.
Yet the one they most despised for her base
    shamelessness,
Was the evil villain's side-kick, the sulky
    villainess.
The cowpokes, silent, spellbound, watched the
    drama seeth and rage,
Until the local woman minced onto the stage.
Now, each eye that beheld her knew this woman
    well.
And silence fell upon the crowd as if by fun'ral
    knell.
A saucy French maid's uniform she wore, as on her
    way,
She lightly tripped across the boards with her tea
    service tray.
The villainess, with pistol drawn, was raging on
    with ire
As the local lass, unheeding, crossed the line of
    fire.
A shot rang out! Down went the maid! The silver
    tea set flew.

A shocked and silent audience's hearts went
    crashing too.
"What have I done?" the villainess asked rhetoric'ly.
"What have I done?" she asked again, as she
    prepared to flee.
One cowpoke jumped up boldly, despite the smoking
    gun,
And broke the dreadful silence with, "I'll tell
    you what you done."
Breaking with emotion, the cowboy's voice grew
    sad,
"You jist shot the best damn whore that this town
    ever had!"

JOB BENEFITS

"How'd you come to be a puncher?"
This here dude ast this old hand.
"Is it 'cause ya like t' see the sky
And the critters on the land?

"The feel of sun upon yer back,
And of bein' yer own boss.
And like life free and easy like
A' 'lopin' on yer hoss."

"It's that an' more," the puncher said
A'swallerin' back a smile.
"But I'm inclined t'wards gittin' lost
'Thout no marker ever' mile.

"I ain't too much good at walkin',
An' in order to survive,
A fellers got to git around
But I never learnt to drive.

"My past is kinda pintoed up
So I guess I back the hope
My prospects will be better on
The right end of the rope.

"Some brains is took to git ahead
These days you will allow.
The only thing I got to be
Is smarter than a cow.

"I hankered to be tall and slim,
An' so it seemed to me
If I got way up off the ground
I'd escape some gravity.

"These boots I wear's the clincher
It's a fact you can't deny
Jist think of all the effort saved
Not havin' shoes to tie."

COMMENTS ON COWBOY POETRY CRITICS

"Deep from the wellsprings of culture." "From hidden
   seeds these anthems have sprung."
"Subtle roots nurture wildflowers." "From complexity
   plain words are wrung."

"Ta dum, Ta dum pounds the meter." "Shallow
   predictable rhyme."
"Dogie doggerel stampede." "Bunkhouse bard pap."
"Ho hum, Humpty bumpkin time."

A caution to those who'd dismiss us;
   or praise our work as sublime
And heap too much praise, or too little,
   upon a cowpuncher's rhyme.

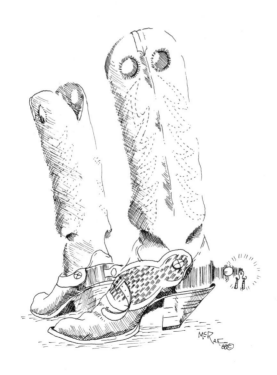

THINGS OF INTRINSIC WORTH

Remember that sandrock on Emmells Crick
Where Dad carved his name in 'thirteen?
It's been blasted down into rubble
And interred by their dragline machine.
Where Fadhls lived, at the old Milar Place,
Where us kids stole melons at night?
They 'dozed it up in a funeral pyre
Then torched it. It's gone alright.
The "C" on the hill, and the water tanks
Are now classified, "reclaimed land."
They're thinking of building a golf course
Out there, so I understand.
The old Egan Homestead's an ash pond
That they say is eighty feet deep.
The branding corral at the Douglas Camp
Is underneath a spoil heap.
And across the crick is a tipple, now,
Where they load coal onto a train,
The Mae West Rock on Hay Coulee?
Just black and white snapshots remain.
There's a railroad loop and a coal storage shed
Where the bison kill site used to be.
The Guy Place is gone; Ambrose's too.
Beulah Farley's a ranch refugee.

But things are booming. We've got this new school
That's envied across the whole state.
When folks up and ask, "How's things goin' down there?"
I grin like a fool and say, "Great!"
Great God, how we're doin'! We're rollin' in dough,
As they tear and they ravage The Earth.
And nobody knows. . . or nobody cares. . .
About things of intrinsic worth.

Wallace and Clinton McRae represent the third and fourth generations of a pioneer ranching family on the Rosebud Creek in southeastern Montana. Their ancestor John B. McRae came to the Miles City region in 1882 and began ranching in 1886.

Wally is a graduate of Montana State University; served as a navy line officer; is a charter member and past chairman of the Northern Plains Resource Council; is a bank board chairman; and is an active member of a community theater group in his home town of Colstrip as an actor, director, lyricist, and playwright. He has had two previous books of poetry published; *"It's Just Grass And Water"* and *"Up North Is Down The Crick."* He and his poetry have been featured at The National and various state Cowboy Poetry Gatherings; and the National and Border Folklife Festivals. He was a featured poet in the Cowboy Poets film and is a recipient of the Governor's Award for the Arts.

Clint grew up on the family ranch, Rocker Six Cattle Company, and has an art degree from Western Montana College. His artistic talent is expressed in such various art forms as stained glass, pottery, drawing, painting in various media and saddle-making. He spends most of his time filling in for his dilettant father on the Rocker Six Ranch. He plans to get married in the spring of 1989 if his ranch activities allow enough time.